The Empowered Entrepreneur

Conquering Core Wounds for Business Breakthroughs

by Ranchelle Van Bryce

Also by ICN Publishing

Light From the Shadows, Enriching the Lives of Others

Take Action "NOW" – No More Waiting

THRIVE: Transformative Strategies for Entrepreneurs

Sparks of Hope: Shooting for Success

CATALYZE: Sparking Change for A New Tomorrow

MASTERY: Harnessing the Power of Expertise

UpLevel Your Future: No More Hiding

Hardcover ISBN: 978-1-0692071-5-9

Paperback ISBN: 978-1-0692071-4-2

EBook ISBN: 978-1-0692071-3-5

Front cover image by Milica Jelenic

Edited by Kim Dietrich, www.kimdietrich.ca

ICN INC.

ICN Publishing | www.icn-publishing.com

The Empowered Entrepreneur

Conquering Core Wounds for Business Breakthroughs

By Ranchelle Van Bryce

Forward

I would first like to thank my parents. I believe that we decide who our parents are going to be so that we can have the experiences required in order to expand to our most empowered self. The journey here on Earth is not for the faint of heart. I am forever grateful for every experience that I have had with my mom and dad and in no way do I blame my parents for my experience as their daughter. I do believe that as a parent, we do the best we can with what we have. I truly am a product of my environment and would not switch any of my experiences for an easier life. Dad, you introduced me to my very first personal development books by Deepak Chopra and Wayne Dyer. Thank you for your insight to know this is what I needed at the tender age of 15.

Next, my incredibly awesome children, Mackenzie and Jacob. I have told you many times how grateful I am that you chose me to be your Mom. Although this is cliche, you have made me a better person by allowing me the opportunity to be your Mom.

Mackenzie, when I found out that I was pregnant with you, I made the decision to ensure that you would never feel unloved or unwanted by me and that I would be as transparent as I could be with you about the trials and tribulations of being a human being. Your self assuredness in who you unapologetically are has been inspiring to me.

Jacob, when you decided to join me in this lifetime, I felt so honoured with your light heartedness and ability to love so deeply. I would watch you play for hours in the backyard waving your magic wand, fighting dragons and saving your castles. You taught me how to let go and allow my imagination to take over.

To Leo, my son from another Mom. You have taught me persistence and dedication at an even deeper level. You have shown me that it doesn't matter what other people think or say, when you have a dream and you're willing to pursue it at all cost; it is possible. Your focus is inspiring.

To Rob, my life partner. Thank you from the depths of my soul for being who you are. You are the first man in my life to not put up with my B.S., to demand more from me than what I thought was possible, to challenge me when I needed it the most and for your unwavering support in my dreams. It was because of you that I was able to see how my wounds and fears were showing up in my life. You were the perfect mirror for me as I was healing. I love you and I see you.

To you, the reader. Thank you for saying yes, to buying the book. If you resonate with the title, then I know that you are on a healing journey and acknowledge your courage and fortitude.

Ranchelle ♥

Contents

Introduction

When was the last time you asked yourself, WHAT DO I WANT?

I want you to think about that for a minute. What do you really, really, really, want? Not what you would settle for, BUT what you really want.

Are you afraid to admit you want more than what you currently have because you can't possibly work any harder than you already are? Do you feel like all your business strategies have lost their impact? Are you weighed down by imposter syndrome? Or are your relationships suffering because you feel completely maxed out and stressed out.

Do you feel like something is missing but you can't figure out what it is?

If you want something different, I understand. I've been in that place and have come out the other side, making my way through a journey of deep personal growth and intense professional learning – one that at times brought me to my knees – and I emerged stronger and more confident than ever.

You can get there too, but the path won't likely look the way you think it will.

Most entrepreneurs think that they just need a new strategy to help get what they want, but my 24 years in business, and my journey of personal development, has shown me that strategies don't work long-term – until we address our underlying mindset.

I will never claim to have "a proven formula for success," but I have helped countless women step into more in their businesses and relationships. If you're willing to commit to looking within so you can move forward, you can grow as well.

Thank you for joining me here – and congratulations on committing to looking at your life in a whole new way. This is going to change everything.

Ranchelle ♥

Chapter 1: Sometimes You Have To Fail First

My entrepreneurial journey began as the first woman in Canada to buy a Curves for Women Fitness Franchise, and I owned and operated a total of 8 Curves franchises between 2000 to 2010 when I shifted into business consulting. In 2012, I formed a highly successful marketing agency that operated for 5 years, and then in 2018 my passion for coaching compelled me to shift focus. At that point, I launched my current company, Ignite Your Success Coaching & Consulting.

When I was running Curves, and winning awards, anyone looking in would have seen a female entrepreneur running a highly successful 7 figure business. I was working super-hard, operating at lightning speed, and only taking the occasional 'working' vacation. I made all the sacrifices I thought were necessary to run a 'successful' business.

The truth is, I was a mess. I felt completely alone – physically unwell and really unhappy. I had success on the outside, but it came at the cost of my health and my relationships. No matter how much money I earned, and no matter how hard I worked, I still felt like I wasn't enough.

I hammered away at the 'problem' – buying into the marketing formulas of countless gurus who hooked me with the underlying message that I wouldn't be 'enough' until I bought their solution. I wasn't smart enough, pretty enough, professional enough... you name it.

When I look back, it's no surprise that none of their solutions helped in the long term.

Two Words That Changed My Life

One day stands out in my memory. I opened up to another successful woman – someone I really respected – about how much I was struggling. Her two-word response changed my life: she said "me too".

I couldn't believe this incredible woman felt exactly the same way I did. And then I realized there must be other women who felt the same as well.

Since then, I have talked with scores of female entrepreneurs and found echoes of how I felt – they didn't feel they were enough. They constantly compared themselves to others. They were full of envy and felt like imposters. Scores of 'highly successful' women were immobilized because what they felt on the inside was keeping them from leading their best lives.

Like me, these women invested time and money into strategies for building professional success, only to end up with results they couldn't sustain.

Our stories helped me see that I didn't need to work harder or get a new strategy. I needed to change the way I was looking at everything. I needed to shift my mindset.

Building A Different Kind Of Success

My journey of personal growth and development led me to a new place, one where I draw on the skills of my professional background and the lessons of my own spiritual development to help others move forward. Today my definition of success looks nothing like what it did years ago. What drives me today is a desire to change the way women look at their businesses and lives. **Success for me today is all about ease and flow.**

I help passionate, enterprising women in competitive industries build profitable businesses so they can create the lives they desire. I guide them through mindset, skillset, and spiritual development so they can show up as their best selves in every circumstance.

What sets me apart from other coaches though is that I don't draw on a business background alone. Personal development and spiritual learning have shown me the importance of self-awareness – that only when we're able to address our underlying fears, will they stop holding us back.

> ***"You cannot solve a problem with the same mind that created it." Albert Einstein.***

If you want to live a life of ease and flow, a life of personal and professional abundance where you don't have to sacrifice your health or relationships, I encourage you to stick with me and learn how integrating spirituality and authenticity into your day to day can help you build the life you desire. *It is possible to create everything you want in your business and life without having to work harder or sacrifice your health and your relationships.*

Today I am magnificently obsessed with guiding women to live their best lives through a process of personal and professional learning that is founded in self-awareness. The women I work with become aware that all parts of our lives are interconnected – that what we learn in one area helps us grow in all of them. It is possible to get what you really, really, really, want – whether that is professional success, physical health and wellness, or thriving personal relationships. It's possible to find the 'something different' that you are yearning for. It just takes a commitment to look within. I encourage you to read on!

Chapter 2: Core Fears

As a strong, independent woman, you're likely not afraid of much, right? What if I told you that your fears are motivating you a lot more than you realize, and that your fear of failure – whether you're conscious of it or not – may really be holding you back.

Have you wondered why you might be afraid of failing? Are you afraid of success? Is it just that you're fearful of taking risks, or is there something else going on? You see, not only is fear a deep feeling that's very hard to move through, but they are also wrapped up in our beliefs. But where do our fears come from?

Somewhere along the path of our experience, we assigned a negative meaning to fear when something happened or when we made some kind of mistake. When that happened, our brain became programmed, or wired to remember that. So even if you don't have a specific, conscious memory of the particular situation or 'failure' your neural network stored it all those years ago.

So what happens is, when you're facing something that seems a little bit unknown, your body starts to respond in a similar way – telling you "I don't want to go here into this space of making a mistake. I am afraid of failing because this bad thing or feeling will happen. It could have been something really simple that you tried when you were a child that didn't work out, or an experience you had when someone laughed at you or bullied you. It may not seem that serious when you think back on it, or it may not even stand out in your memory, but your brain remembers it very clearly and it has a lot of power over you.

A Core Fear Lightbulb Moment

Let me give you an example: When I was growing up, I really didn't like to be teased, you know, and as an adult, same thing I didn't really like to be teased and for the longest time, I thought it had something to do with when I was bullied as a child, or maybe something to do with my parents not allowing teasing, but a few months back I came upon this memory that triggered an intense feeling of humiliation. I was in grade two and had just finished a gymnastics class at school. That day I had worn tights and a skirt and when I came out of the change room after gym class, I had forgotten to put my skirt back on. There I am, seven years old, and I came out of the changeroom and one of my classmates, a young boy, started pointing at me and laughing – because I didn't have any pants on.

So when this memory came flooding back to me during a coaching session, I paused, I asked for the grace to move through the moment and I had a lightbulb moment. I realized that the fact I don't like to be teased is wrapped up in this memory of the humiliation I felt standing in front of my grade two class with no pants on. But it goes even deeper than that for me.

When I am afraid to make a mistake, or I am procrastinating with something, it's because I'm afraid that I am going to do something and someone's going to point their finger at me and laugh at me, and I'll be humiliated. If I am wrong, or if I do something wrong, people are going to laugh at me and I will feel bad. So my fear holds me back, even when I'm not aware of it.

We all have fears like this and they can stop you from trying new things or from exploring different avenues and approaches. They can be debilitating, causing procrastination and self-sabotage. But we don't start out in life with all our fears. As I explained, they came from somewhere and part of what we can do now is we can look at our current situation with a new lens – through the eyes of you as an adult versus the eyes of you as a child.

What I think is really helpful is to understand fear more fully at its base level so we can understand how pervasive it can be in our lives today.

We're all born with two basic fears – fear of loud noises and fear of falling – and then we have other fears programmed into us in childhood by our family members – our parents, our grandparents, even our great-grandparents. We develop six basic fears: fear of poverty, criticism, loss of love, aging, failing health, and death. Depending on our background and the experiences we have growing up, some fears become more prominent than others – and they end up affecting everything we do.

A Fear-Fairy Tale

Maybe you had a family member who grew up during the 1930s facing extreme poverty and despair. They will have unconsciously programmed their fear of poverty into other family members, passing on their fear of not having enough, their fear of running out, even their mistrust of institutions that should be trustworthy. You likely don't consciously think about the fear you've inherited – it's just part of who you are, running beneath your surface, influencing your actions and decisions, and holding you back in ways you aren't even aware of. Maybe you say things like, "I can't afford that" or "Money doesn't grow on trees" or "You have to work hard to make a living". Pretty harmless right? Well, not exactly....

How does your fear of poverty affect you?

You set out to open your own business, and excitedly told your parents about it, and they got quiet. They asked – "Isn't that risky? After all, you need to be careful financially. How will you feed your family if things don't work out? How will you be able to retire comfortably without a pension?" So you worried a little, but you're a confident woman, so you forged ahead and opened your business – after all, you were full of hopes and dreams!

But then despite all your hopes, things got hard, didn't unfold how you expected, and you started to get a little nervous, because now there's no guaranteed paycheque. Maybe it seems really difficult to attract new clients, or to charge enough to 'make ends meet'. Maybe your cash flow isn't quite where you want and the bills are piling up. You get unconsciously triggered and your fear of poverty takes over your mental background chatter: how will I ever make enough to succeed, how will I buy supplies next month, pay my mortgage, buy groceries, or send my kids to university?

As fear spins in your mind, a couple other guests arrive at the party – your limiting beliefs and your core wounds – and then you start to panic, spiral, and search for an answer. You convince yourself that you just need a system or a strategy or a skill set – you need a solution to fix the problem, which you have pinpointed as a cash flow problem or a pricing problem or a new client problem....

You don't see that your fear itself is the problem because it's holding you back from doing the things you need to do to create the cash flow, and charge higher prices, and attract more clients.

Unless you slay the dragon that needs slaying – your fear of poverty and all the limiting beliefs and the core wounds that come with it – your result will always be the same. You'll have ups and downs, but you'll always return to the same place because you won't have addressed the fears, core wounds and limiting beliefs driving your thoughts and beliefs.

You don't need another system or solution – all the answers are right inside you. And the first step involves taking a really good look at your fear, because it is possible to get to a place where it doesn't have a grip on you. I want that for you, and I'd like to show you HOW to get there, because although information and education are great, they're not much use if we don't know how to apply them to our lives.

We're going to look next at how to apply, integrate and embody all this information in your own life, by looking at how our fears have created limiting beliefs, and how those really hold us back.

"The greatest barrier to success is not external competition, but internal fear. Conquer that, and you've won half the battle." Ranchelle Van Bryce

Chapter 3: Limiting Beliefs

We have talked about how our fears often sit just below the surface and hold us back without us even being aware. Today I'd like to share about how our fears lead to limiting beliefs, which also hold us back.

My clients often tell me they feel like they're meant to have more but can't possibly DO more because they're pushed to their limit and completely tapped out. And I get it, because that was my story as well – always searching for a solution that would bring success. The turning point for me was learning that there was nothing wrong with me. I didn't need a solution. The path to success started with confronting my fears and limiting beliefs – and now I help other women do just that so they can move into self-empowerment as well.

We don't see the world as it actually is. Our perception of the world depends on our

beliefs. We see everything through the lens of our beliefs.

Here's a good example of how one of my beliefs put limits on my life. My parents were entrepreneurs and one of my memories is that they said: you can have fun when your work is done. That became one of my core beliefs – a very limiting one, because, as I'm sure you know, when you're an entrepreneur, your work is never really done.

So, although I ran a "highly successful" business, my limiting belief that "fun comes after work" led me to put off rest, exercise, and socializing, and it led me to neglect my personal relationships. I worked myself into burnout, unhappiness and a failed marriage...not exactly a description of success! My limiting belief kept me from experiencing a balanced and fulfilling life, but when I shifted that belief, everything changed.

I remember the day my house phone rang (you know this is a long time ago because I still had a landline!) and answered a pretty huge call from my mom, who took care of all the finances for our Curves business. She called to tell me that we (myself, her and my Dad) had just hit the million-dollar mark in our business. It was a pretty epic moment because that was a success goalpost for me. I had told myself the story that when we hit the million-dollar marker, we would have arrived – we would be 'a success'. We had all bought champagne in anticipation of this event, so we cracked a bottle on our ends of the phone and toasted our success together. After we hung up I ran a bath to have a luxurious soak with my glass of bubbly while I waited for my husband to come home. And then I laid back in the tub and I thought – a million dollars.... And I didn't feel any different. I felt hollow and empty, sitting alone by myself in my house with no friends to call to celebrate – because I had poured every bit of my energy into being 'a success,' driven by the belief that fun has to come after work.

As I laid back and let the tears flow, I thought to myself, "I have given up so much for this glorified dollar amount, and here I am, by myself, unhappy." And it was then that it started to dawn on me that money was not going to make my life better. I'd arranged my whole life around running the business – sure I made sure I was there at the end of every day to pick up my kids, but other than that, the business came first and I came last.

I hadn't let myself take a vacation away from work for years. I travelled FOR work, but the business always came first. So after that lightbulb moment in the tub, an opportunity came up for me to have a little getaway when a new friend invited me to join her on a summer solstice yoga retreat in New Mexico. I had set things up so that I could stay in touch with my kids and with work from my cell-phone while I was away, and I was all set to take a little 'me' time....but the Universe had other plans.

I like to say that nothing happens "to you." Everything happens "for you." And when I look back on that yoga retreat I can see that what happened was part of something bigger that I needed to happen in my life. You see, when we ascended into the mountain range where the retreat was being held, I lost cell service – and I completely panicked. I had no idea how I would be able to call my daughter on her birthday, let alone stay in touch with everyone in the business throughout the week. I had convinced myself – and everyone else in the business – that things couldn't run without me. And short of a brief phone call from the main office to let everyone know I would be entirely out of range, I was forced to go off-grid for the entire week.

Given that my beliefs were: fun comes after work, and my business couldn't run without me, the circumstances taking place seemed like the end of the world at that moment in time. But, over the course of that week, I underwent a shift in my thinking and started to really realign my beliefs as I examined what really mattered to me in my life.

Common Limiting Beliefs

We don't always have to be backed into a corner or up against our wall to examine our beliefs and figure out what isn't working for us. We can decide to figure out what's going on beneath the surface and work on shifting it – before the Universe forces the issue for us!

It can be challenging to go through the process of figuring out our limiting beliefs, but it can also be lots of fun! Let's look at a few common limiting beliefs around running a business – see if you can spot any that you believe.

- Business is hard.
- It's hard to attract clients.
- It's hard to make money.
- Money doesn't grow on trees.
- There isn't enough time to do what needs to be done.
- Customers and staff are high maintenance.
- I have to put everyone else's needs before my own.
- I like what I do but I hate the sales and marketing part of my business.
- I have to sacrifice time, and my relationships with others to be successful.
- If I want to succeed, I have to put myself last.
- I will be happy 'when'...

What do you imagine we create by holding beliefs like these? What kind of energy do you think we attract to our business with them? Think about what I created in my life and my business with my limiting beliefs. We create circumstances that support our beliefs – and then we stay stuck in them. And no matter how hard we try to change the situation, it won't change ... until we change the underlying beliefs.

If you're not sure what your limiting beliefs are, a great thing to do is to start taking a look at your groundhog days – those moments you find yourself experiencing over and over. There's such gold in them because they point directly towards your limiting beliefs.

And once you identify the lessons that keep showing up again and again, you can work on shifting them. This can be challenging work to do on your own because it's difficult to see beyond the lens of our own beliefs. The important thing for you to know is this:

When we are stuck, or confused or not feeling good, there is some sort of limiting belief influencing the way that you're thinking. The good news around that is, when you start to adjust your thinking, you're going to begin to change everything.

This is how it's played out in my life: the moment I have confusion, the moment I don't feel good, I've learned to stop and say "Wait a minute, I am not in my truth. I am believing something. I'm in a limiting belief of some sort that's causing the confusion. I may be stuck in some sort of limiting belief that was programmed into me during my childhood." Where it came from isn't as important as moving into awareness of the belief so you can start to shift it.

Uncovering the lens that you're viewing things through can have such a huge impact on how you show up in the world – in your business and your personal life – everywhere. It'll give you the opportunity to move yourself out to a 30,000-foot level view and be an observer of your life. In that place you'll start to see how your beliefs, thoughts, and emotions are affecting you, where you're taking things personally, how you're showing up and why you're showing up that way. You'll start to see the truth behind why you do what you do.

I am not sure if we ever 'eliminate' our limiting beliefs. What we can do is figure out what they are – become aware of them – and then start to move through them differently. I have found through different modalities that the thought or belief is still there; however, it has way less "spiciness" to it and it doesn't affect me in a negative way.

Groundhog Days

Identifying our "groundhog days" – the circumstances or situations we find ourselves going through repeatedly – can be a great way to figure out what our limiting beliefs are. Start paying attention to themes that show up over and over for you – to things you seem to keep coming up against.

You can also use the questions below as a starting point for tapping into your limiting beliefs.

- What are the difficulties or problems or challenges that keep showing up for me?
- Are there any common themes or similarities that keep showing up?
- What do you think might be holding you back? Why do you think the same lessons keep showing up?
- Can you see any beliefs that you could let go of here?
- Ask yourself: How can I think differently about this thing in order to have the things that I desire?
- Ask yourself: How can I use a different lens to shift my perception and change my reality?

It is your power to think that determines your state of living. But it is also within your power to take action, even in the midst of your discomfort and fear. As my mentor told me a long time ago, **to create the life we want, and the business we want, we need to get comfortable with being uncomfortable.**

This can be challenging work, but the great thing is, you don't have to do it all at once, and you don't have to do it alone. You can find a mentor or a coach who can help you look at what you're creating through a different lens.

In the next chapter we're going to scratch a little deeper beneath the surface and talk about how our early experiences can lead to core wounds and what that creates in our lives.

Chapter 4: Core Wounds

Thanks for sticking with me on this journey of staring down our core fears and limiting beliefs. I hope you've found some value in what you've read so far – and I want you to give yourself a pat on the back. This work is uncomfortable, AND it's super empowering! Getting to a new level of awareness where you see how you're showing up and why you're showing up that way – it changes everything.

I want to take a look next at the power of our early life experiences, how they lead to core wounds, and what that creates. Growing up, as we have fears programmed into us, we form beliefs around them. And then, we have impactful experiences that confirm those beliefs and leave us with core wounds. Typical core wounds are abandonment, rejection, or loss of love, and they influence how we think, feel and behave – without us being aware of them at all.

I’ll tell you how they played out for me.... I grew up in an alcoholic home and my experience with my mom was that she was hyper-focused on our dad’s behaviour and my sister and I being rewarded or punished based on our behaviour. Punishment meant you were ignored, no longer paid attention to, which energetically taught me “I have to do things a certain way in order to be loved, so there must be something wrong with me. I'm not smart enough. I'm not pretty enough. I'm just not enough to be loved for myself. I suck.”

And then I went out into the world and experienced evidence of that over and over again. It became my core wound.

I would sit in class knowing the answer to my teacher’s questions, but I was too afraid to speak up because I felt like there was something wrong with me. When the teacher did call on me I’d panic, which only confirmed my feeling that “I suck”.

As evidence piles onto our core wound, it gets continually reinforced. Then, we grow into adults and step into business, and it shows up there as well. Maybe you have a cool business idea and you are sure people are going to flock to your door. When they don’t – perhaps because of a lack of sales and marketing skills – your core wound of “There’s something wrong with me” steps up and all you see is, “People aren't buying from me because I'm not smart enough, not pretty enough, just not enough. I suck." And then you don't address the real issue, which is a lack of skill in sales and marketing, which is an easy fix!

Our core wounds affect how we respond in situations, how we perform, and how people receive us. We project our core wounds and present ourselves in a way that energetically projects our feelings about ourselves at people. Our words may say "hey this product or service is great," but our energy says otherwise, and people pick that up unconsciously.

How you show up on a regular basis – in all areas of your life and your business – is related to your core wounds and that's why it's so important to understand them. When you start to work on this stuff – on your shadow self – and you gain an awareness of your core wounds, you will also start to respond versus react. You will stop perpetuating the cycle and start confidently showing up in the truth of what you have to contribute. Now, what is really important in our healing is to recognize that *it is our interpretation of the experience that causes the wounding.*

Working on Your Shadow Self

Working on our shadow self – the stuff beneath the surface – is challenging work. You're not really meant to do this work on your own – because it's hard to see beyond your own thinking. It's difficult to see what's going on beneath your own surface that contributes to your thought patterns and the way you operate in the world. It's when you reach out and hire someone to do this work with you that you can really start to make some significant shifts. That was definitely the case for me.

My core wounds of abandonment and rejection continue to show up for me today, but they have much less of an emotional impact on me now than they did before, because I hired a coach to help me. Together we worked on my shadow self, and I was able to move into new levels of awareness.

Doing this work has shifted things for me, so I don't take things as personally now. I've stopped telling myself the stories that were based on my core wounds. When things happen now, I no longer automatically give them meaning around abandonment rejection. But I had to do a lot of work to get there.

Let me give you an example of how my core wounds used to show up for me. My second marriage ended after I discovered that my husband had been unfaithful to me. He'd not just had one affair – it was several, both in person and online – over many years. My first response – my conditioned response, based on my core wounds of rejection and abandonment – was to make it about me. And that's where I went at first – giving it the meaning that our marriage sucked, or that I sucked, or that there must be something horribly wrong with me sexually – something which was perpetuated by societal beliefs and by people saying things like “I thought you had a really good sex life,” as though that was the reason for his infidelity. Thankfully, because of the work that I had done, I didn’t stay there long.

I could have made everything about my core wounds of rejection and abandonment, and attribute everything to them – to think at a core level that this happened to me because I suck – but fortunately, I was able to shift my perspective. I was able to look at our relationship more objectively, and to see that while I had contributed things to the relationship that weren’t perfect, his cheating on me had nothing to do with me.

He didn’t cheat on me because there was something wrong with me. He did what he did because there was something inside him that led him to his decisions. He, himself, had a set of beliefs that led him down this path. You don't get into a relationship with someone and cheat on them all the time unless something is broken. Today that’s probably not a word I would use, but at the time, that’s where I was.

So rather than making it all about his rejecting and abandoning me, I was instead able to release the sting of abandonment and rejection, look at how I participated in the deterioration of the relationship and take a radically honest look at how I was showing up in the relationship. And there were some valuable lessons in that. Once I was able to get past my core wounds, I was able to start healing. I want to add, in complete transparency, that this process took a few years for me. This was not an overnight process. My abandonment and rejection wounds were deep.

Core Wounds in Business

If you have core wounds around abandonment and rejection, they can affect you profoundly in your intimate relationships. But they can easily show up in business as well – particularly when it comes to sales and marketing. If you have abandonment and rejection issues, you won't want to make sales phone calls. You'll be shy and just really have a lack of self-confidence and self-esteem around making sales calls. That's a common one that shows up for people.

I remember a time when my core wounds showed up for me in business. I was doing my very first really big event, in 2020 and though the ticket sales were successful at the end of 2019, they dropped off as we got close to the event in 2020 – right when we expected them to pick up. Because of the personal development work I was engaged in at the time, I became aware pretty quickly that the event performance had something to do with my mindset. I dug into that a little bit and started to see that I had tons of fear around doing the event. I realized I had thoughts like:

- What if it didn't work out?
- My intention was to have two hundred women there, and what if we couldn't make that happen? What would that say about me?
- What if I disappointed my sponsors?
- What if the people collaborating with me were disappointed in me?
- What if people came to the event and it completely sucked?
- What would everyone say?

All of those thoughts were around rejection. I was telling myself a story: if things went a certain way, everyone would be mad at me. Everyone would think that I sucked, and then they'd all be gone. I was operating from the fear that they were going to reject me, and that would lead to abandonment. People wouldn't want to be in a relationship with me, wouldn't want to be friends with me, and wouldn't want to come to my events.

I realized that my thinking had sent me into freeze mode. I had stopped promoting the event. I stopped talking about it and I had stopped messaging people about coming. Once I saw what was going on, I realized I had to really shift my thinking. I did that by fully stepping into everything I feared.

I asked myself what was the worst thing that could happen if the event was a flop? I made myself consider the worst possible scenario:

- My collaborators would be upset and not want to partner with me anymore.
- The sponsors would never want to sponsor another event again.
- The participants would talk about me and about how much the event sucked.
- And everyone would think that I sucked.

And once I considered all these possibilities, I asked myself what else could be possible? And here's what I came up with:

- I would find someone else to collaborate with, because I'm really good at convincing people, showing them my vision, and making them want to be around me.
- I would find new sponsors.
- I would find people to come to my next event.

I saw that I didn't have to give everything the meaning that I was giving it. I could just go out and do what I do best, which is promote other people and promote the event. So I made a new decision about what is possible. And I found evidence that was contrary to what I was worried about. I found new evidence to support me and what I was doing.

I realized that I didn't need to give it the meaning that I was giving it.

Our core wounds of abandonment or rejection can profoundly affect us as business owners. If you have that core wound, why would you put together a marketing strategy that could lead to abandonment and rejection? Why would you do a podcast and put it out there for the world to hear and judge you and think that you suck? Why would you post on social media? Why would you want to have marketing conversations or try to make sales conversions? If you're worried about abandonment and rejection, then you won't create a marketing funnel or a sales funnel. You won't initiate generative conversations, and you won't put yourself out into the world.

And without all those things, you have no chance of success.

But – once you're able to move into awareness of those core wounds, and the fears and beliefs around them, you can start telling yourself different stories. You can start making different decisions. You can change the meaning that you give things. You can't do that though, without being in awareness – which we're going to talk about in our next chapter.

5

Chapter 5: The Gift of Self Awareness

So far we've talked about our core wounds, core fears, and limiting beliefs and we've explored how they're all interconnected – how they work in tandem to keep us stuck. With them running the show, we keep repeating the same patterns of behaviour that hold us back in our lives and our businesses.

When we are in that place where worry, doubt, and fear are at the forefront of our mind, we are operating in the past. We're existing in our memories and our fears, limiting beliefs and core wounds are in the driver's seat. And while we're operating from the past, it's impossible to stay centred in the present. Instead we end up existing within the negative thoughts that are part of our old personal self.

The great news is, we can create something entirely different once we're able to let go of that past conditioning – both our own conditioning and the conditioning that came to us all the way from our ancestors. We can step into the future and start telling a new story based on all our new awarenesses instead. This is an exciting place really! It's a place where anything is possible, and the sky is the limit, so congratulations on getting here!

What comes next can be a little scary. Being in a place where you're stuck in old patterns – but you've realized you need to make a change, but you aren't sure what to do next – can be uncomfortable. This is where the real work begins!

But take heart – what I have come to see is that the ease and flow you are looking for is on the other side of the growth that's about to happen!

I hope you've done a little work on the writing I suggested back in Chapter 3 – the exercise I shared on writing about your groundhog days can be really helpful with getting a start on uncovering some of your patterns and stepping more fully into self awareness. If you didn't get a chance to, I encourage you to go back and do so!

I'm guessing if you're still here that you ARE willing to move into awareness, and that's awesome, because now I'd like to talk about what to do with what you've come up with.

Here's a recap of a few key points:

Typical **core fears** that most humans possess fall into these categories: fear of poverty, criticism, loss of love or rejection, aging, failing health, and death.

And our **core wounds** typically boil down to these three things: I'm not enough, I suck, I'm not smart enough.

The most common **limiting beliefs** out there are generally one or more versions of the following: relationships take a lot of work, no one will ever love me, business is hard, I can't afford that, you have to work really hard to be successful.

When you're able to step into awareness of your own core fears, core wounds and limiting beliefs, you start to see how they affect your life And from there, you can make the decision to start changing them.

As I shared in previous chapters, I have fears of criticism, poverty, abandonment, and rejection, and I've battled with core wounds and limiting beliefs about not being good enough – that sprung from those core fears. And I've shared with you about how they affected my life at the event in Red Deer I had planned that wasn't going the way I wanted and attendance looked like it would likely be super low. First I went deep into my fears: "Oh no! There won't be anyone at my event. People are going to think I did a terrible job! I'm not a good leader. I'm not enough. I suck."

Because of the work I've done to become more self-aware though, I was able to pause and take another look. I asked, "what else is possible here?" I realized I could fall flat on my face and choose to not take it personally – to be okay with it. I looked at my fear that the speakers and sponsors would think I'm not good at what I do and saw that what that was really about was my fears of criticism, of people thinking I suck, of people leaving me.... And then I zoomed way out....

The beliefs that I created are just decisions. I created them and I can recreate them. I can stop listening to my fears/beliefs/wounds, look at the evidence in front of me, and make a new decision about what to feel/think/believe.

I looked at the evidence of how I'd run events in the past. Yes, maybe for this event, attendance would be low, but maybe no one would be disappointed. What if everyone was really happy with the way the event went? After all, an event is about the experience. And when I host an event, it's always an experience, because of how I show up naturally as who I am – inclusive and connected, in an energy of love and kindness, giving everyone the space to show up as who they are. I'm aware of who doesn't feel like they belong and I pair them up with others. It doesn't matter if there's 50 people there, or 150 people. My skill set is still there and I will still show up in the beingness of who I am.

I looked at all that evidence and decided to think something different like: "this event is going to be fantastic. It's going to be an experience like none other!" And that shifted me into a whole different energy.

When we become aware of how our core wounds, fears and limiting beliefs are running the show, we can pause, look for evidence, and make a new decision. Quite simply, you can identify your old belief, decide on a new belief, and then look for evidence to support it.

This work requires radical honesty with self. It requires us to look underneath – at our shadow selves – at all our ugly patterns and the toughest parts of ourselves that are sometimes easier not to acknowledge. It requires us to shine a light into our darkest places, and it's not an easy thing to do.

Thankfully, I had a coach who helped me through it. I'm super grateful for what I learned from doing that work with my coach. At the time, however, I didn't feel quite as positive!

We are 100% responsible for everything in our lives.

I would say the most significant step for me with building awareness came when I realized that I was 100% responsible for everything. I remember being in a coaching session when I said to my coach that I didn't know what my limiting beliefs were, and I got really angry with him when he told me that, yes, I did know. He just responded by saying “look around you, Ranchelle. Everything that you've created is a result of your beliefs.”

Everything. And so I started to look around. And I became aware of all of the amazing things, right, my kids, my relationship, brains, all the things I had achieved. But I also then became aware of my limiting beliefs. And it was, it was, it was hard, because it was a rush of, of all the struggles that I had, and all the obstacles and challenges and everything. So I would say this step for me was to accept that I was 100% responsible for everything. And it was so easy to accept the cool stuff, the cool stories. Yeah. It wasn’t so easy to accept the darker side, the shadow self.

It's easy to accept that we have created all the good stuff in our lives, but it’s tough to accept that we are also responsible for all of that negative stuff as well. We’re responsible for the patterns that are keeping us stuck.

It was really tough for me to make that realization and look around and realize that yeah, I was responsible for all the good stuff, but, but for the shit as well. And you know, how those moments when you have those reactions that if you can stay there, you can be aware that the reaction is giving you information and telling you something.

We're conditioned to like, not feel. Don't be angry. Don't be sad. Get over yourself. Right? Turn that frown upside down. But if I don't know how to look at something radically, honestly then we can't see the truth of ourselves. We can't face our shadow selves.

Shining a Light of Truth on Ourselves

The truth is, I am very kind, AND if I'm in a confrontation and the right trigger exists, I can be very conniving. I am both kind and conniving. I am both impactful, influential, and manipulative. And until we really become aware of the shadow self, we can't expand into our fullest selves. Once we do our shadow work though, and accept the darkest parts of ourselves, then we can get to a place where we can expand the brilliant side of ourselves and fully step into our divine selves. Our shadow work is all about shining a light on the truth of ourselves – shining a light on our shadow selves.

The shadow work I did while looking back at my second marriage was very powerful. It gave me so much information about myself. I realized that in my marriage, every decision was motivated in trying to ensure my husband would love me, not because I loved him. There is a big difference between the two – and the shadow truth was that I manipulated our relationship because I wanted him to stay with me.

We are conditioned not to look at those kinds of things, but when we can step into radical honesty with self, it is a gift. Doing that work and coming to the awareness helped me to really start to heal in my current relationship. I saw where I was trying to manipulate within this relationship – and how insidious that pattern was. I realized that my partner, who loves to ride motorbikes, didn't have one now because of me. Because my love language is quality time, and he knew how I would react if he went off on his own on a bike – with irrational childish anger based on my fears around abandonment and rejection – he had chosen not to pursue something he loved.

I was able to come to that realization because of the shadow work I had done, and it was incredibly powerful for me, because it meant that I could make a different choice. I could look at the evidence and decide – holy shit, he doesn't have a bike because of me. I don't want to be that girl – and I could make a different choice.

Shadow Work is Healing Work

Seeing your shadow self is all about shining a light on yourself so you can move into self-awareness. Without that light – without the self-awareness it brings you – you cannot heal and move through the patterns that are keeping you stuck. That's the gift of awareness. And we get there so much more effectively when someone else is helping us get there. When you work with someone who can mirror back to you what they see, and show you where to shine that light, they can guide you and give you hints or clues about where to look. They can ask you the right kind of questions so that you know where to look. And they can help you do so without getting lost in the guilt or shame that invariably comes up when we look at our shadow selves, because guilt and shame will stop you in your tracks.

When we look at our shadow selves, we can so easily become mired in guilt and shame. And we can't expand and create and manifest something new if we're experiencing guilt and shame.

If you're doing this work on your own you will have guilt and shame come up – and that’s not the purpose of doing this work. We step into radical honesty of self, into self-awareness, so we can have compassion and empathy for ourselves. We take an unsparing look at ourselves so we can know ourselves better – not so we can beat ourselves up. This is about knowing ourselves so we can love ourselves. And we need help to do that because it's scary to do on our own.

The work you put into building awareness will help enable you to make different decisions and create different outcomes. Getting radically honest with yourself takes courage and commitment, but you can get to the other side. That’s when you can truly expand and step into the full expression of you – into your superpowers – where your natural gifts truly show up.

Chapter 6: Tapping into Your Superpowers

Do you realize how powerful you are? You have superpowers. REALLY - YOU DO! In fact, we all do, but sometimes we need a little help recognizing what they are before we can fully step into them. That's what I'd like to turn our attention to next – because I am all about sharing what I've learned with you to help you thrive in your body, your business and your relationships!

I want you to think about a person you admire – someone you think of as a high achiever. Chances are they're a gifted individual. You might even call them a winner. Here's the thing though, that person isn't a winner because they naturally have more gifts than the rest of us. They became the way they are **because** they claimed their natural gift. They took their gift out of its wrapping and found a way to use it.

We all have natural gifts – some of which we may not really be aware of. Sometimes our gifts are difficult to spot **because** they come to us so naturally. Maybe you know your gifts, or maybe you need some help uncovering them....and I can help with that!

I came to an awareness of my own gifts both by working with a coach and doing a lot of personal reflection. I looked at some of the things my parents used to say to me that I took on as criticisms, (even though they may have meant well). They used to say, you're such a great starter. But you're not a very good finisher. And I had been telling myself that story for years. I believed that I couldn't finish anything. But when I started to question it, I came to see that it wasn't actually true. I do finish things. But, because of how I process things, they often end up looking very different than when I started them.

So then I started to look at other observations people had made to me about myself – friends, colleagues, peers – and I made a list of all the things that I'd ever heard about myself, both positive and negative, and then looked at, like the common denominator.

What I came away with is that I'm a great starter – I am naturally gifted at generating ideas. They come to me all the time, in all kinds of places. And that realization was huge because I came to see what I had thought was a personal failing as one of my greatest gifts.

I did another exercise with my coach at the time where I was to imagine what I would do if I had all the money in the world. If I had $22 million dollars and all my needs were taken care of – what would I do?

When I was asked that question I knew immediately that I would do coaching and consulting. I would help women build their businesses, and I would teach sales and marketing. Through that exercise I became aware of my natural gifts. I came to see that I am naturally a business builder. It doesn't matter what business is, I just love to get in there, get things going, and have so much fun.

I'm also a natural connector. In the work environment I love networking, storytelling, and listening. I enjoy doing those things. They come naturally to me – they're my gifts – my superpowers you could say. So if you're looking to get more clarity about your natural gifts, think about the things that feel easy for you, the things that when you see others do poorly, you can't understand it because it comes so naturally to you.

Think about what you would do if you had all the money in the world and you could do what you really enjoyed. What would that look like for you? As you sketch that mental picture, you'll start to uncover some of your natural gifts.

The Gift of Judgments and Criticisms

Think as well about the judgements or criticisms that others have made about you. These can be an indicator to you of your natural gifts, as well as when you find yourself in judgement of someone else. Any time a judgement comes up it can be an opportunity to pause, shine a light back on yourself and see what information about you exists in that judgement. Perhaps it's an area where you can grow, but it may be a hint at one of your superpowers.

Think about the things that people compliment you on. Maybe you're someone who is super-organized, and that's just who you are, maybe that's your gift. We can even call it your superpower. And there are opportunities to use your superpower in your life and your business. Maybe somebody needs to know how to get organized, and you have a way to present information in a way that they'll understand it.

Think as well about where you've been judged in the past by someone and it's left you feeling shame about some aspect of your personality or your abilities. Where have people criticized you? What stories have you been telling yourself in those places? How could you begin to shift those stories and tell yourself something new? There are all kinds of tools available to help with sorting through the stories you've been telling yourself – Human Design is a great one – but it can also be super helpful to work with a coach. It's tough to wade through all that information and get a clear look at what's underneath without having someone guide you through the shadows.

I'd love for you to start uncovering the gifts that you've never even opened – to become open and willing to receive your gifts, your natural talents, and your superpowers. They're not something you need to chase after – you just have to move into awareness of what they are.

Everyone has natural gifts. The people we think of as superstars, or gifted, are just ones who've managed to identify and harness their gifts. They've stepped into their superpowers and run with them. So what holds us back from having a 'successful' life isn't necessarily that we don't have gifts – it's that we're not clear on them, or we're not willing to receive them.

I've noticed how difficult it is for some people to receive, and how often it's that inability or awareness of how to receive that holds us back. What about you? When people give you compliments, what do you do? Do you receive them or dismiss them? If you were to manifest your deepest desires tomorrow, would you be open to receiving them? Are you willing to accept your superpowers – your gifts?

It can be an incredible boost to your confidence when you step into your natural gifts, and that can spill over into your business in a way that will really grow your success. Getting in touch with your gifts – identifying them and coming to clearly see their value will help you grow in clarity and confidence with them and then you'll also become more comfortable with charging more for your services.

The Biggest Gift of All

The one we all have in common, is our ability to be in touch with our Divine self. When you're in touch with who you truly are – with your "I Am-ness" – nothing is out of reach. When I've asked Divine to show me where my gifts lie, what I noticed is that it often comes to me in the form of someone else sharing something about me, and it's made me pause and go, "Oh, I never thought of that!" So you can ask your Divine self to show you your hidden gifts and how to access them.

Along the way, it's important to get as clear about your desired outcomes as you possibly can, and it's as simple as asking for it, and then being willing to listen and receive. Maybe that clarity will come to you through meditation, while journaling, or even in conversation with others – what's important is that you listen and keep asking: "can I get just even a bit more clarity?"

Clarity is so valuable, because with clarity comes confidence – and that helps us as we make decisions about the path we want to move forward on in life. When you have a very clear destination in mind, and you know that you are meant to get there, you can stand firmly in your determination to get there; you can map out the steps you need to take to get there, and you can begin to get really intentional about moving towards your ideal life.

So start by getting really clear about your intention, how you want to feel, what do you want your epic life to look like? And then by listening to your intuition – your Divine Self – on a regular basis, and asking for clarity, you'll be led forward.

It's just up to you whether you're willing to receive your gifts, and whether you're willing to receive the guidance available to you from your intuition – from your Divine Self. It's entirely up to you whether you're willing to take the next steps to moving forward with all that information. What's really important that you know is that you do not have to do it alone. In fact, chances are that you will be more likely to achieve your outcomes – that things will become more clear more quickly – if you work in partnership with a coach. That has been what I have experienced again and again on my learning journey, and that is what I want for you too.

We'll talk more about that in the next chapter!

Chapter 7: Your Pathway to Success

I've shared a lot of information with you so far and given you a lot of ideas on how to tap into the information that's inside of you. That's only the first step on the pathway to success though. The next step – and this one is key – is figuring out how to integrate and embody that knowledge. It's great to read a book and highlight all the key points, for example, but what you do with that information will determine whether it goes from idea to action.

I speak from personal experience with this one. The number of self-help books I have filling my bookshelves is staggering, but I came to see that knowledge, or information, is not enough to effect change in our lives though. It requires something more – and I came to that realization myself when I was going through a really tough time myself back in 2018.

I remember that I was looking through my library of books, looking for something specific to help with what I was going through. Personally and professionally I was in a really terrible place. I was just considering throwing in the towel with my own business and just going out to find a management job in retail, or sales or something, anything – I thought I would just go sell cars or insurance, or whatever. I had been crying and thinking to myself, “I'm done. I'm done fighting. I just give up.” And at that moment, I was compelled to go to my bookshelf, because I wanted to let my mind go. I saw this book about the universal laws, I thought to myself, I don't even remember getting this book, and I’m sure I've never read it or even picked it up before. But when I opened it, I saw that it was full of all kinds of highlights and notations. It had sticky notes all through it, and I had no recollection of ever having read it.

A lightbulb went off in my head at that moment and I realized, my life had been full of working to gain knowledge, but that I had not done anything with that knowledge. And that was the reason why I didn't create success.

So I decided from that moment on anything I read, I would integrate. From there, I stopped reading so much. Because I probably had two hundred books in my library and I wasn’t doing anything with them.

So slowly, I started to go through one book at a time, one paragraph at a time. I went through them in painstaking detail – taking one single paragraph and asking the question, "How can I integrate this today? How can I apply this to my life today? Or where is it applicable?"

I focused on one book in particular that dealt with the universal laws, and I would review no more than a page at the most in one day – carrying it around with me, and asking, "How does this apply to my life? And am I integrating it? I would stay with that chapter until I felt like I had integrated the information in a meaningful way.

Daily Mindset

Once I began to integrate the knowledge into my life, things really started to change for me. I started to build the foundations for the successful life that I had desired, and I started working with clients to try to do the same.

As I worked with my clients in the months that followed I observed that between our sessions, my clients were making progress, but in a 'two steps forward and half a step back' pattern – this was an observation on my part, rather than a judgment. That's one of my superpowers – observing patterns.

When I saw that pattern, I asked myself what the difference was between what they were doing and what I was doing and I saw the missing piece. I was reading and reflecting on short passages of *developmental* information every day and then focusing on how I could integrate them – and I was doing that on a consistent basis, dedicating a short amount of time to this practice every single day.

Something incredible was created as a result of that realization – it led me to create a morning group call because I saw that I could add value to my clients by inviting them into the same type of practice – by facilitating that for them every single day. What I came to see about the impact of the group was this: its power lies in the fact that it presents knowledge by melting it out in little, tiny bits, day by day by day by day. It allows me to share the lessons I have learned in a way that helps my clients thrive in all parts of their lives.

The Pathway to Success

Personal and professional growth is crucial for helping us create big, bold, and beautiful lives, but because we get so busy with our day to day, it often falls to the bottom of our to-do list. That's the beauty of the Morning Mindset Group – it offers a sacred, dedicated space for conscious female entrepreneurs to regularly honour their commitment to personal growth. It's a way for us to begin our days centred in a mindset of awareness, so together we can move towards living our very best lives.

As I write this, the group has been meeting regularly via my membership platform. Each person who joins us comes to the space from a different point in their own personal development, and we all consume information and learn differently; all that to say that what each person gets from out the group is different. I present information and each listener receives whatever they are meant to receive.

It's an informal space with no expectations for anyone who joins. After a quick hello and a bit of an informal chat, I start recording the call and then I flow into that day's teaching. I keep my camera on but there is no expectation for anyone else to be on camera – though some people do and it can help with the flow and channeling of energy. Then I wrap things up after a half hour or so.

What I encourage everyone to do as they begin walking down the pathway to success, is to tap into what feels right for them and follow it. When people first join I always tell them:

You're not meant to immediately grasp everything right away – it will take some time!

With that in mind, I encourage everyone to listen and let the information wash over them. Sometimes that means hanging out in the background of the group listening to the teachings and conversations for a couple of weeks to get a feel for the lay of the land, or perhaps doing some of the background readings I suggest that provide an introduction to the basics that my teachings are based on. I also maintain a private YouTube channel with a library of previously recorded calls and those are available for anyone who wants to get an idea of what things have been recently covered.

As with most approaches to personal growth, there is no right or wrong way. I like to say to my clients: "You can't mess this up. Whatever you are meant to know or understand right now is what you will pick up!"

8

Chapter 8: Embracing Your Empowered Future - The Path Forward

Throughout this book, we've delved deep into the internal barriers that often hold entrepreneurs back from achieving their fullest potential. Now, let's bring it all together and provide you with a comprehensive roadmap to authentic success.

Key Principles Revisited

Before we dive into actionable steps, let's revisit the core principles that form the foundation of becoming an empowered entrepreneur:

1. Your internal landscape shapes your external reality.
2. Self-awareness is the cornerstone of personal and professional growth.
3. Core fears and limiting beliefs can be transformed into sources of strength.

4. Everyone possesses unique "superpowers" that can drive business success.
5. Integration and consistent practice are key to lasting change.
6. Authentic success comes from aligning your business with your true self.

These principles will guide you as you continue on your journey of growth and transformation.

Your Empowered Action Plan

Now, let's translate these insights into a concrete action plan that will propel you forward on your path to becoming an empowered entrepreneur.

1. Confront Your Core Fears and Wounds

- Set aside dedicated time this week for deep self-reflection.
- List out your primary fears (e.g., poverty, criticism, rejection, failure).
- Identify any core wounds (e.g., feeling not enough, unworthy, or unloved).
- For each fear and wound, ask yourself: "How has this manifested in my business decisions?"
- Write a letter to your younger self, offering compassion and understanding for these fears and wounds.

2. Challenge Your Limiting Beliefs

- Create a "belief inventory" by listing out your recurring thoughts about yourself and your capabilities.
- For each belief, ask: "Is this based on fact or fear? What evidence contradicts this belief?"
- Craft new, empowering beliefs to replace the limiting ones.
- Write these new beliefs on sticky notes and place them where you'll see them daily.

3. Cultivate Radical Self-Awareness

- Commit to a daily mindfulness or meditation practice, starting with just 5-10 minutes a day.
- Begin journaling regularly to track your thoughts, emotions, and patterns.
- Set a thrice-daily reminder to pause and ask yourself, "Why am I feeling/thinking/acting this way right now?"
- Seek feedback from trusted friends, mentors, or a coach about your blind spots.

4. Uncover and Harness Your Superpowers

- Reflect on compliments you've received throughout your life and note any patterns.
- Ask five people who know you well what they see as your greatest strengths.

- Spend an hour imagining what you'd do if money were no object and all your needs were met.
- For one week, track which tasks energize you and which drain you.
- Based on these insights, write a "Superpower Manifesto" outlining how you'll incorporate your unique gifts into your business strategy.

5. Integrate Knowledge Through Consistent Practice

- Choose one concept or insight from this book to focus on each week.
- Set daily reminders to pause and reflect on how you can apply this knowledge.
- Start or join an accountability group to support your growth.
- Commit to a daily Morning Mindset practice, either by joining a group or creating your own ritual.

6. Align Your Business with Your Authentic Self

- Revisit your business mission and vision. Do they align with your values and superpowers?
- Audit your products or services. How can they better reflect your authentic self?

- Examine your business model. Does it support your desired lifestyle?
- Create systems that honor your natural rhythms and strengths.

7. Embrace Vulnerability and Seek Support

- Research and reach out to potential coaches who can guide you through this process.
- Join or create a mastermind group of like-minded entrepreneurs.
- Share your growth journey with at least one trusted friend or family member.
- Commit to attending at least one personal development workshop or retreat in the next six months.

8. Celebrate Progress and Practice Self-Compassion

- Create a "Win Jar" where you write down and collect your small victories.
- Schedule monthly "progress parties" where you acknowledge how far you've come.
- Develop a self-compassion mantra to use when you face setbacks.
- Start a gratitude practice, noting three things you're grateful for each day.

Overcoming Obstacles on Your Journey

As you implement these strategies, you will inevitably face challenges and resistance. This is a normal and even necessary part of the growth process. When you encounter obstacles:

1. Return to your 'why': Reconnect with the deeper reasons you started this journey.
2. Lean on your support network: Reach out to your personal board of directors or community of entrepreneurs.
3. Reframe setbacks: Ask yourself, "What can I learn from this? How is this helping me grow?"
4. Take inspired action: Even small steps forward can reignite your momentum.
5. Practice self-compassion: Treat yourself with the same kindness you'd offer a good friend.

Visualizing Your Empowered Future

As you continue on this path of growth and self-discovery, take a moment now to envision the empowered future that awaits you:

Close your eyes and imagine waking up a year from now, feeling deeply aligned with your purpose. You start your day with a sense of excitement and possibility. As you move through your workday, you find yourself effortlessly tapping into your superpowers, creating value with ease and joy. Your business is thriving, not just financially, but in its positive impact on the world.

You navigate challenges with grace and confidence, knowing that you have the inner resources to handle whatever comes your way. Your relationships, both personal and professional, are characterized by authenticity and mutual respect. At the end of the day, you feel a profound sense of fulfillment, knowing that you're living true to yourself and making a meaningful difference.

This future is not just a dream – it's a very real possibility when you commit to the principles and practices we've explored in this book. Remember, becoming an empowered entrepreneur is not a destination, but a lifelong journey of growth and evolution.

The Ripple Effect of Your Transformation

As you step into your power and align your business with your authentic self, remember that your growth creates a ripple effect that extends far beyond your immediate sphere. By doing this inner work and showing up as your true self:

- You inspire others to do the same, creating a more authentic and empowered business culture.
- Your clients and customers benefit from your increased confidence and clarity, receiving higher quality products or services.

- Your personal relationships deepen as you bring more authenticity and self-awareness to your interactions.
- You contribute to a shift in the broader entrepreneurial landscape, demonstrating that success can be achieved without sacrificing well-being or authenticity.

Committing to Lifelong Growth

As we conclude our journey together, I invite you to commit to lifelong growth and development. This means:

- Staying curious and open to new insights and perspectives.
- Regularly reassessing your beliefs, goals, and practices.
- Continuing to invest in your personal and professional development.
- Sharing your learnings with others, as teaching deepens your own understanding.
- Embracing each challenge as an opportunity for growth and self-discovery.

A Final Word of Encouragement

As we close this chapter and this book, I want to acknowledge the courage it takes to look within and commit to personal growth. By engaging with these ideas and considering how to apply them in your life and business, you've already taken significant steps on the path to becoming an empowered entrepreneur.

Trust in your ability to grow, adapt, and thrive. You have everything you need within you to create the success you desire. Your unique gifts, experiences, and perspective are needed in the world. As you continue to do this inner work and align your business with your authentic self, you'll not only transform your own life but also inspire and uplift others in ways you may never fully know.

Remember, your success and personal growth ripple out, creating positive change far beyond what you can see. The world is waiting for your unique contribution. It's time to embrace your empowered future and shine your light brightly.

Thank you for joining me on this transformative journey. I'm excited to see how you'll apply these principles and the amazing things you'll create as an empowered entrepreneur. Remember, this is just the beginning. The best is yet to come!

Now, take a deep breath, connect with your inner wisdom, and step boldly into your role as an empowered entrepreneur. Your journey to authentic success starts now. The world is waiting for you to shine.

Manufactured by Amazon.ca
Bolton, ON

45127912R00048